The Battle of
Yorktown

Events That Shaped America

Sabrina Crewe and Dale Anderson

Gareth Stevens Publishing

A WORLD ALMANAC EDUCATION GROUP COMPANY

Please visit our web site at: www.garethstevens.com
For a free color catalog describing Gareth Stevens Publishing's list of high-quality books and multimedia programs, call 1-800-542-2595 (USA) or 1-800-387-3178 (Canada). Gareth Stevens Publishing's fax: (414) 332-3567.

Library of Congress Cataloging-in-Publication Data

Crewe, Sabrina.
    The Battle of Yorktown / by Sabrina Crewe and Dale Anderson.
      p. cm. — (Events that shaped America)
    Includes bibliographical references and index.
    ISBN 0-8368-3412-7 (lib. bdg.)
    1. Yorktown (Va.)—History—Siege, 1781—Juvenile literature. I. Anderson, Dale, 1953-. II. Title. III. Series.
    E241.Y6.C76   2005
    973.3'37—dc22
                                        2004058189

This North American edition first published in 2005 by
Gareth Stevens Publishing
A WRC Media Company
330 West Olive Street, Suite 100
Milwaukee, WI 53212 USA

Produced by Discovery Books
Editor: Sabrina Crewe
Designer and page production: Sabine Beaupré
Photo researcher: Sabrina Crewe
Maps and diagrams: Stefan Chabluk
Gareth Stevens editorial direction: Mark J. Sachner
Gareth Stevens editor: Monica Rausch
Gareth Stevens art direction: Tammy West
Gareth Stevens production: Jessica Morris

Photo credits: Corbis: cover, pp. 5, 12, 13 (top). 14, 18, 20, 24, 26, 27; National Archives: p. 10; North Wind Picture Archives: pp. 4, 6, 7, 8, 9, 11, 13 (bottom), 15, 17, 21, 22, 23, 25.

Printed in the United States of America

1 2 3 4 5 6 7 8 9 09 08 07 06 05

Contents

Introduction

In 1776, thirteen British colonies in North America united to declare themselves an independent nation. This building in Philadelphia, now called Independence Hall, was where the Declaration of Independence was signed.

Revolution in the Colonies

In 1775, the first shots were fired in the American **Revolution**. The war, which lasted until 1781, was a long struggle for thirteen **colonies** in North America that were ruled by Britain. The people of the colonies were fighting hard to win independence from Britain and form a new nation. On July 4, 1776, years before the struggle was over, the colonies declared themselves a union of independent states: the United States of America.

The Long Struggle

Britain was a powerful nation, however, with a mighty navy and a large army, and the British were prepared to fight to keep the colonies as part of their **empire**. The Americans had only a small army and very little money to wage a war, but they kept fighting.

At Yorktown

By the summer of 1781, the war was in its sixth year. A large British army had entered Virginia followed by an American force. The British moved onto a **peninsula** in the eastern part of Virginia and seized the city of Yorktown. The Americans stayed nearby until more troops arrived by land and sea to help them.

Encircling Yorktown, the Americans, led by George Washington, trapped the British army, which was led by Charles Cornwallis. On October 19, 1781, after a battle lasting several days, the British surrendered.

A monument to liberty stands at Yorktown today. It is a reminder of the important event that took place there.

After the Battle

The American success at Yorktown was very important for the future of North America. Yorktown was the last major battle of the American Revolution. Soon after, Britain began pulling its troops out of its former colonies. Less than six months later, Parliament (the British **legislature**) voted to stop the war and negotiate a peace **treaty** with the Americans. The United States had won its independence.

In Our Hands

"The present moment will decide American independence. ... The liberties of America and the honor of the Allied Armies are in our hands."

George Washington, commander of the American Continental Army, Yorktown, September 30, 1781

Chapter One

The Revolution Begins

Relations with Britain

Throughout the 1600s and into the mid-1700s, the British colonies in North America sent food products, such as wheat and fish, to Britain and bought manufactured goods in return. Both the colonies and Britain prospered from this trade. In other areas, Britain mostly left the colonies to look after themselves. Colonists could choose their own local government officers and members of colonial legislatures.

Taxes and Protests

In 1764, however, the British government decided the colonies should start paying more **taxes** to Britain. A new law, the Sugar Act, created a tax on certain goods shipped

Crowds in Boston protest against the Stamp Act, a tax law that came after the Sugar Act. The Stamp Act and other tax laws angered the colonists, who believed the taxes were unfair.

into the colonies, so when colonists bought the goods, they paid an extra amount that went to the government.

The Sugar Act was the first of several laws creating taxes and controlling the colonies' trade. Many colonists, calling themselves **Patriots**, protested the new laws. They did this mostly by not buying the taxed goods. They also held public protests, destroyed shipments of taxed goods, and attacked tax officials. In response, the British government sent soldiers to stop the protests.

The British rulers were angry, but the colonists were even angrier. **Delegates** from the colonies met in Philadelphia in 1774 to discuss what they should do. At this meeting—the First Continental **Congress**—the colonists declared Britain had no right to tax them. They decided to form **militia** units and train the units to fight.

The Battle of Lexington and Concord

At this time, although there had been violence, the British army and the Patriots had not yet fought a real battle. In April 1775, however, the real fighting began. At Lexington, near Boston, Massachusetts, British soldiers fired at a small militia force, killing several colonists. The British went on to Concord, where Patriots killed and wounded several British soldiers. The British then suffered heavy **casualties** as they marched back to Boston. The fighting signaled the beginning of the American Revolution.

During the American Revolution, militia members left their families to fight the British whenever they were needed. Militiamen were not professional soldiers—they were farmers, doctors, or anyone who was available.

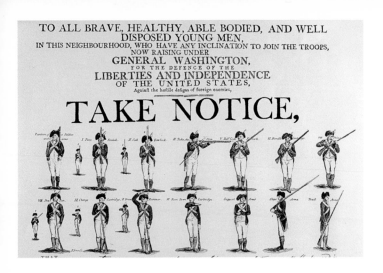

Forming an Army

A few weeks later, on May 10, 1775, colonial leaders met in Philadelphia for the opening of the Second Continental Congress. The delegates decided the colonies would have to defend themselves against the powerful British army.

Militia units played an important role, but the colonies would need their own professional army. They agreed to form a combined force, which they named the American Continental Army. In June, George Washington from Virginia was asked to command the force.

This poster encouraged men to sign up under General Washington and fight in the American Revolution.

The Battle of Bunker Hill

Washington quickly went to take command of the Patriots outside Boston. Before he arrived, however, there was another battle in the area, when the British attacked the Massachusetts militia across the river from Boston. In the

George Washington (1732–1799)

George Washington was born to a wealthy Virginia family. He joined the Virginia militia and fought with the British in the French and Indian War. Congress later picked Washington to lead the Continental Army because of his military experience and his character. He guided the Americans to victory and became a national hero. After the war, Washington retired to his plantation, Mount Vernon, in Virginia. He returned to public life in 1787 and was elected the first U.S. president in 1789. He served two terms before retiring again in 1797.

Battle of Bunker Hill, on June 17, 1775, the British pushed the militia back but suffered very heavy casualties.

The Continental Army Grows

The fighting near Boston had persuaded many colonists to take the side of the Patriots. Men flocked to join the army in Massachusetts. By March 1776, the Americans had surrounded the British army inside the city. Before the Patriots could attack the British, however, General William Howe—commander of the British forces— put his troops on ships and left the city by sea.

In April 1776, Washington moved his base from Boston to just outside New York City. In July 1776, the British moved to Staten Island, also near New York City.

This illustration of Boston in 1774 shows the harbor full of British warships. In 1776, the British soldiers in the city boarded ships and left before the Patriots could attack.

The Declaration of Independence

Meanwhile, Congress had moved away from the idea of a peaceful settlement with the British. On July 2, the delegates voted for independence. Just two days later, on July 4, 1776, Congress approved the Declaration of Independence, which declared that the colonies had become "free and independent states."

Delegates from all thirteen British colonies signed the Declaration of Independence (right). The document said the colonists were determined to rule themselves.

Setbacks for the Americans

In late 1776, after several battles, Washington was forced to abandon New York City to the British and escape across New Jersey to Pennsylvania. His army was now only a few thousand men.

Washington won some battles in 1777, but the year brought more setbacks. The British took over Philadelphia, where Congress was based, and the delegates had to flee the city. At the end of 1777, Washington moved his army into winter quarters at Valley Forge, west of Philadelphia. His soldiers spent a miserable winter with little food or warm clothing.

Good News

In early 1778, the Americans received good news. In February, France decided to take the American side in the fight and signed a treaty of **alliance** with the new United States of America. The Americans could now count on getting important financial and military help from the French.

Also in early 1778, conditions improved at Valley Forge. More supplies arrived, and a German officer named Friedrich von Steuben joined Washington's army. Von Steuben introduced some better training methods that made the soldiers more disciplined and more professional.

Cold and Confusion at Valley Forge
"Poor food—hard lodging—cold weather—fatigue—nasty clothes—nasty cookery . . . why are we sent here to starve and freeze?. . . Here all confusion—smoke and cold—hunger and filthiness."

Connecticut army surgeon Albigence Waldo, describing Valley Forge in his diary, 1777

Soldiers huddle around a fire at Valley Forge during the winter of 1777–1778.

Chapter Two

The Road to Yorktown

Patriot women in South Carolina captured British messengers and searched for hidden documents. Intercepting the enemy's messages was an important job during the war.

Return to New York

The American alliance with France alarmed the British government. In the summer of 1778, the British ordered their forces to leave Philadelphia and return to New York City, where they would have a safer base. Washington placed his army at different points around the city so he could keep an eye on the British.

The British Move South

Three years of fighting in northern regions had produced no breakthrough. Sir Henry Clinton, the new commander of British forces, was ordered to invade the South instead. The British thought they would have more success defeating the Patriots in the South, where they believed they would find more **Loyalists** to help them.

Early in 1780, Clinton sailed south from New York with 8,000 British soldiers. By April, they reached their first target: Charleston, South Carolina. In a disastrous battle for the Patriots, Clinton forced them to surrender the city. The Americans lost 5,400 soldiers, 4 ships, and all of their weapons and ammunition. It was a terrible blow.

Clinton returned to New York City with about half his army. He left the rest in the South under the command of Charles, Lord Cornwallis.

George Washington was the overall commander of all Patriot forces from early in the war until the end. He also took direct command of the American Continental Army, but other generals, such as Nathanael Greene, led other Patriot armies.

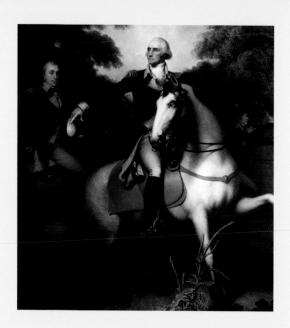

The British forces in North America had several overall commanders during the Revolution. First was Thomas Gage, who led the British at Lexington and Concord and at Bunker Hill. In 1775, he was replaced by William Howe, who had overall command until 1778. Howe was succeeded by Henry Clinton, who held the post until 1782. Like the Americans, the British had other generals who were in command of armies in the field. One of these was Charles Cornwallis, who commanded the British army at the Battle of Yorktown.

(Top) George Washington before the Battle of Yorktown. (Bottom) Charles Cornwallis.

In the South

In October 1780, Washington sent Nathanael Greene to reorganize the American army in the South. The Patriots then had several clashes with Cornwallis's army in North and South Carolina.

In April 1781, Cornwallis decided to lead his army into Virginia, joining forces with another 5,000 British troops. A Patriot force of about 1,200 had also reached Virginia in April, sent by Washington from New York. The Patriots were led by a young Frenchman, the Marquis de Lafayette, who watched the British movements but kept a safe distance.

Making a Base

Cornwallis then received orders from Clinton to secure a base with a good port in the Chesapeake Bay area. Clinton was

Gilbert du Motier, Marquis de Lafayette (1757–1834)

Marie Joseph Paul Yves Roche Gilbert du Motier, Marquis de Lafayette, was an orphan by the age of twelve. He came from a long line of soldiers and joined the army in France at the age of seventeen. In 1777, Lafayette went to America to fight for the Patriots. He was an able officer, and he also gave huge sums of his own money to help win the Revolution. After the war ended, Lafayette returned to France. In 1825, he was invited on a triumphant tour of the United States, where crowds greeted him in every state. He died in France but will remain forever an American hero.

considering sending British ships to Virginia to fetch some soldiers so he could use them for a new attack in the North.

In late July of 1781, Cornwallis chose Yorktown as his port. His troops began reaching the town at the beginning of August. Lafayette followed close behind—he knew he had to stay close enough to make problems for the British, but he avoided risking a battle that could have destroyed his force.

Determined to Skirmish

"Were I to fight, I should be cut to pieces, the militia dispersed, and the arms lost. Were I to decline fighting, the country would think itself given up. I am therefore determined to skirmish, but not to engage too far."

Marquis de Lafayette, letter to George Washington from Virginia, 1781

This street in Yorktown has buildings preserved from the time of the battle in 1781. Cornwallis chose the port town because it had a deep harbor that could be used by large ships.

Chapter Three

The Siege and Battle

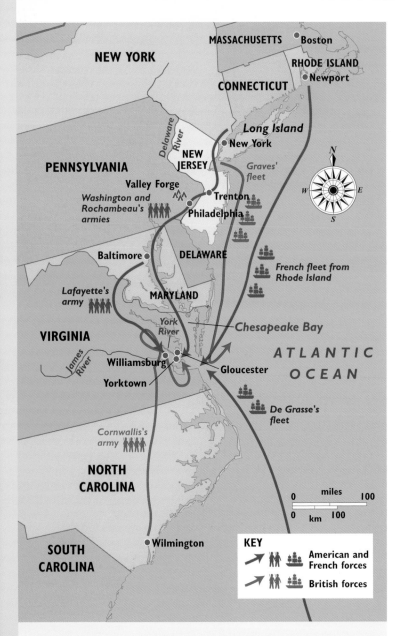

This map shows the movement of troops and ships toward Yorktown, Virginia.

A Difficult Position

In moving to Yorktown in the summer of 1781, Cornwallis had followed his orders to secure a port. He had placed his forces in a difficult position, however. They were on a narrow peninsula where they could be easily surrounded and trapped. The best hope for the army was to be rescued by British ships.

News from France

Washington was still up north, watching Clinton's army in New York. In the middle of August, Washington received important news. A large French fleet, carrying about three thousand French soldiers, was on its way to Chesapeake Bay to help the Americans.

Washington decided he could safely leave just part of his army near New York to watch Clinton. Washington planned to take the rest—along with French forces led by General Jean Baptiste de Rochambeau—to the South. He could then use these soldiers, plus those arriving on the French ships, to defeat Cornwallis in Chesapeake Bay.

Ships and Soldiers Arrive

At the end of August, the French ships under the command of Admiral François de Grasse arrived near Yorktown. The troops were unloaded and went to join Lafayette's army at Williamsburg. De Grasse then managed to fight off the British ships sent by Clinton from New York.

In September, more French ships arrived from Rhode Island. They brought **artillery** that could be used to carry out a **siege**. By late September, Washington and Rochambeau's men had joined up with Lafayette's army at Williamsburg.

While the Patriots were assembling, the British at Yorktown had been busy, too. They were digging **trenches** and building **redoubts** where artillery could be placed.

A British warship is destroyed outside Yorktown in 1781. French ships defeated the British fleet that came to rescue Cornwallis's army.

Missed Opportunity

"[I said] we should get into the Chesapeake to [help] Lord Cornwallis and his brave troops if possible, but that I was afraid the opportunity of doing it was passed by, as doubtless De Grasse had . . . barred the entrance against us, which was what . . . we ought to have done against him."

British Admiral Samuel Hood, in a letter to a navy colleague, 1781

Yorktown in 1781

Before the Revolution, Yorktown was a prosperous port of a few thousand people on the southern bank of the York River. Its main street ran parallel to the river and held the county courthouse, the town's largest church, several taverns, and the shops of tailors, silversmiths, and other craftspeople. The town had many warehouses that stored tobacco, grown on nearby farms, to be shipped abroad. The siege in 1781 destroyed most of Yorktown, however, and it never fully recovered. Only about 250 people live there now, and much of the town is part of the Colonial National Historic Park.

The Patriots Arrive at Yorktown

On September 28, Washington ordered his combined forces to march to Yorktown. By the next day, the Americans and French formed a rough semicircle around the British troops.

Washington's army camped about one mile (1.6 kilometer) from the British base at Yorktown. From there, Washington and his officers planned a siege.

The British Position

Cornwallis's men had been building two sets of trenches. The outer ones were about 1,200 yards (1,100 meters) from the city. The inner trenches were only about 300 to 400 yards (275 to 365 m) outside Yorktown. When the American and French forces arrived, Cornwallis pulled his men back to the inner trenches. He figured that by giving up this land without a fight, he would lose fewer soldiers. By pulling back, however, Cornwallis just made the Patriots' work easier— they would have less ground to capture.

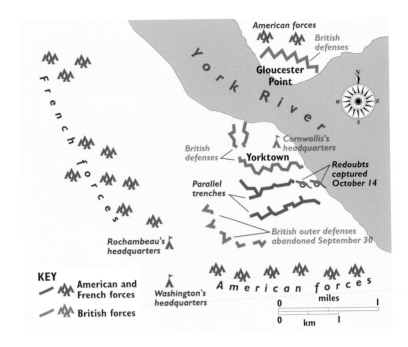

Cornwallis was heavily outnumbered, with only about 8,000 men compared to a combined American and French force of about 17,000. Worse, many of the British were sick and exhausted from marching, and only a few thousand soldiers were well enough to fight.

The American Position

Washington planned to surround the British and force them to surrender. The Patriots began to dig trenches parallel to the British **fortifications**. From there, they could aim their artillery at the British cannons. Then they could dig new trenches even closer, allowing the guns to hit the town.

By October 6, the French and American allies had almost completed a deep line of trenches about one mile (1.6 km) long and about 600 yards (550 m) from the British line. They were ready to begin the siege.

French and American forces surrounded Cornwallis's army at Yorktown and moved in closer as the siege progressed. With no ships to rescue them, the British were trapped.

19

General Washington prepares to fire the first cannon at the British position on October 9, 1781.

Opening Fire

On October 9, the Patriots' artillery was in position. Washington took the honor of firing the first gun, and thousands of shots followed. By the end of the first day, the allies had shot more than 3,600 **shells** at the British. Only at night, when the allies' bombardment lessened a bit, could the British return fire.

Firing on the Town

Many shots hit the town as well. The few civilians who were left in Yorktown went to the riverbank to hide there. The allies aimed some shots at the bigger, finer houses, believing that the British officers were likely to be there. Cornwallis had to move his headquarters twice because of the shelling.

Getting Closer

Cornwallis knew he was in serious trouble. "Against so powerful an attack," he decided, "[we could] not hope to make a very long resistance."

The Americans soon began digging trenches just 300 yards (275 m) from the British lines. The diggers came under fire from British artillery, but they kept working. On the night of October 14, the allies captured the two last redoubts held by the British army. By the next morning, the Americans and French had completed the new line of trenches. The two redoubts they had captured anchored that line.

British Response

Early in the morning of October 16, when it was still dark, the British tried to strike back. Soldiers rushed forward to take the American trenches nearest the British lines. They hoped to spike the cannons there, which meant filling the barrels with dirt so they could not be fired. The allied soldiers fought back, however, and the British were forced to retreat.

On the night of October 14, the allies attacked and captured the British redoubts.

A Desperate Move

Cornwallis had one last trick left. He hoped to send his army across the York River to Gloucester, defeat the small American force there, and escape. Some of the troops did make it across the river on October 17, but a violent thunderstorm forced the remaining boats to turn back.

Terms of Surrender

Cornwallis finally concluded that he had no hope. On October 17, he sent a junior officer to discuss surrender terms with Washington. The British wanted to surrender with honor, which would mean they could fly their flags and carry their weapons as they marched out of Yorktown. The Americans, however, had been forced to surrender at Charleston the year before without such honor, and so they refused the British this privilege.

A British officer comes to the Patriot line at Yorktown waving a flag of truce. Behind him a drummer beats a drum to request a "parley," or talks with the other side.

Reasons to Surrender

"Under all the circumstances, I thought it would have been wanton and inhuman to the last degree to sacrifice the lives of this small body of gallant soldiers, who had ever behaved with so much fidelity and courage, by exposing them to an assault, which . . . could not . . . succeed."

Lord Cornwallis to Henry Clinton,
explaining his decision to surrender, 1781

On the afternoon of October 19, 1781, the surrender at Yorktown took place, and the Battle of Yorktown was over. Despite the battle's importance, the losses at Yorktown were fairly light. About 500 British were killed and wounded, and the Americans and French had about 260 dead and wounded.

The Ceremony

Cornwallis felt ill and did not take part in the surrender ceremony at Yorktown. He sent his second-in-command, General Charles O'Hara, to give up his sword to the opposing commander. O'Hara tried to give his sword to Rochambeau, who pointed him to Washington, the allies' commander. Since Cornwallis had sent his second-in-command to surrender, however, Washington directed O'Hara to General Benjamin Lincoln, Washington's second-in-command, to take the sword.

The British army then marched out with flags covered. The French army in their crisp white uniforms lined the west side of the road, while the more ragged Americans lined the east. The British filed through, stacking their weapons in a field.

Chapter Four

After the Battle

Free and Independent
"His Britannic Majesty acknowledges the said United States . . . to be free sovereign and independent states."

Treaty of Paris, 1783

The End of the War

Although it was not the last battle of the American Revolution, Yorktown was the last significant one. As Lafayette wrote soon after the battle, "After this attempt, what English general will undertake the conquest of America?" He was right. In 1782, the British sent delegates to Paris, France, to work out a peace treaty with American officials.

It took a long time to work out a treaty that both sides agreed on. After much arguing, American and British diplomats signed the Treaty of Paris on September 3, 1783. The treaty granted the independence of the United States and set the boundaries of the new nation. It gave the United States the right to territory from the Atlantic Ocean to the Mississippi River.

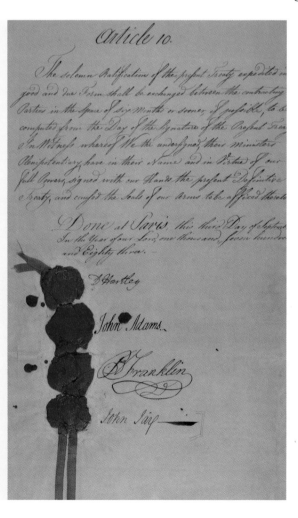

The Treaty of Paris was signed in September 1783. You can see the names of two famous Americans, John Adams and Benjamin Franklin, on the last page of the original document.

Government for a New Nation

A new nation needs a new government to run it. Congress had drafted a plan for government called the Articles of Confederation, but the plan didn't work for long. Under this plan, the government was not powerful enough to make the former colonies work together as a nation. Many leaders worried that the United States would fall apart.

In 1787, a group of U.S. leaders decided to get rid of the Articles of Confederation and draft a new plan of government. They wrote the U.S. Constitution, a set of basic laws for the nation that is still in operation today.

According to the Constitution, the United States needed to have a president to lead the nation. In 1789, the first U.S. president was chosen—George Washington, the former commander of the Continental Army and widely admired hero of the American Revolution.

A More Perfect Union
"We the People of the United States, in Order to form a more perfect Union, establish Justice, insure domestic Tranquility, provide for the common defence, promote the general Welfare, and secure the Blessings of Liberty to ourselves and our posterity, do ordain and establish this Constitution for the United States of America."

Constitution of the United States, 1787

This engraving shows George Washington speaking at the Constitutional Convention in 1787. At the meeting, U.S. leaders worked out a new plan of government for the nation.

Conclusion

An Important Battle

When the American Revolution started back in 1775, few people on either side believed that American forces could defeat Britain's powerful army and navy. It often looked as if the Patriots would be defeated.

Compared to some battles in the American Revolution, the Battle of Yorktown was fairly small. Its impact was huge, however, because the American victory over Cornwallis's army caused the British to give up the fight. The British realized that the colonists were determined to win their independence. So from thirteen small colonies, a new nation was formed that soon expanded across the continent. Today, it is one of the most powerful countries in the world.

Yorktown Today

The Yorktown battlefield and town are now part of the Colonial National Historic Park in Virginia. A visitor center just outside the town greets people coming to visit the site. It has exhibits that describe the battle and the participants. Visitors can walk the grounds and see where some of the key events in the battle took place. They can also see some of the buildings from the 1780s that still stand in Yorktown. Among these buildings is the one where the surrender was negotiated. The house of General Thomas Nelson, which was struck by several cannonballs during the siege, also survives.

A Yorktown Myth

A well-known story says that, when the British army marched out to surrender at Yorktown, a British band played a tune called "The World Turned Upside Down." The world certainly had been turned upside down—after all, the most powerful empire on Earth was surrendering to an army it had defeated many times before. The story, however, is probably untrue. None of the participants in the surrender—on either side—mentions the tune in accounts of the ceremony.

Time Line

1764–1767	British government passes Sugar Act and other laws imposing taxes on the colonies.
1774	September 5–October 26: First Continental Congress.
1775	April 19: Battle of Lexington and Concord.
	May 10: Second Continental Congress begins.
	June 17: Battle of Bunker Hill.
1776	July 4: Congress approves Declaration of Independence.
1777	September 26: British occupy Philadelphia.
1778	February 6: Americans and French sign treaty of alliance.
1780	May 12: British capture Charleston, South Carolina.
1781	April 25: Cornwallis leaves North Carolina for Virginia.
	August 1: Cornwallis reaches Yorktown, Virginia.
	August 19: Washington begins march toward Virginia.
	August 30: De Grasse's fleet arrives off Yorktown.
	September 5: Battle between British and French fleets off the coast of Virginia.
	September 28: Washington's army arrives at Yorktown.
	October 9: Americans open fire on Yorktown.
	October 17: British ask to discuss terms of surrender.
	October 19: British surrender at Yorktown.
1782	British government sends delegates to Paris, France, to work out peace treaty with U.S. officials.
1783	September 3: Treaty of Paris is signed.

Things to Think About and Do

A Continental Soldier

Find out what you can about the life of a soldier in the American Continental Army. Imagine you are one of those soldiers, and write a journal of a few days in your life during the American Revolution. You could be a soldier at Valley Forge, on the march, or at Yorktown during the battle.

A New Nation

When the thirteen colonies joined together to become a nation in 1776, their leaders had many issues to think about. They had to set up a national government and create a currency (system of money). They also had to decide what powers the national government should have and what powers should belong to individual states.

Imagine that you are setting up a new nation in today's world. Think about the kind of challenges you would face, and write about your ideas of what would make a good system of government.

Glossary

alliance: agreement between groups or countries to support and defend each other. Those who take part in the agreement are "allies."

artillery: large, heavy guns such as cannons.

casualty: person who is wounded, killed, or missing in battle.

colony: settlement, area, or country owned or controlled by another nation.

congress: meeting. The name "Congress" became the name of the U.S. legislature when the United States formed a government.

delegate: person chosen to represent a group at a meeting.

empire: large territory under the control of a powerful nation.

fortification: structure built as protection from an enemy.

legislature: group of officials that makes laws.

Loyalist: American who wanted the colonies to stay under British rule.

militia: group of citizens organized into an unofficial army (as opposed to an army of professional soldiers).

Patriot: colonist who supported the American Revolution. More generally, a patriot is loyal to and proud of his or her country.

peninsula: piece of land jutting out into the water but connected to the mainland on one side.

redoubt: small fortification where artillery was placed.

revolution: overthrowing of a government and setting up of a new system of government.

shell: case that contains explosives and is fired from a gun.

siege: military operation in which attackers surround a target and either attack it or keep it trapped in order to force a surrender.

tax: sum of money charged by governments on purchases, property, or income and used to pay for public services or governing costs.

treaty: agreement made among two or more nations or peoples.

trench: ditch cut in the ground to protect soldiers from enemy fire.

Further Information

Books

Burgan, Michael. *George Washington* (Profiles of the Presidents). Compass Point, 2002.

Hakim, Joy. *A History of US: From Colonies to Country* (Volume 3). Oxford University Press, 1999.

Marcovitz, Hal. *The Declaration of Independence* (American Symbols and Their Meaning). Mason Crest, 2003.

Stewart, Gail. *Life of a Soldier in Washington's Army* (American War Library). Lucent, 2003.

Web Sites

memory.loc.gov/ammem/bdsds/intro01.html Library of Congress Web site about the Continental Congress and how the Constitution was written.

www.nps.gov/colo/ National Park Service Web site for the Colonial National Historic Park has details about Yorktown, the battle, and historical background at the "in depth" link.

www.pbs.org/ktca/liberty/index.html Web site of the PBS documentary series on the American Revolution has information about Yorktown and many other aspects of the Revolution.

Useful Addresses

Colonial National Historic Park
National Park Service
P.O. Box 210
Yorktown, VA 23690
Telephone: (757) 898-2410

Index

Page numbers in **bold** indicate pictures.